DESTRUCTIVE LIES

Healing

T·R·U·T·H

31 DAYS OF ENCOURAGEMENT FOR PATIENTS AND CAREGIVERS TO FIND STRENGTH, PURPOSE AND PEACE IN HEALTH-RELATED TRIALS

BY
M. A. PASQUALE

ISBN: Softcover 1983723738
        eBook   9781386071761
EAN: Softcover 978-1983723735

http://hopewordslife.com

PREFACE

This book intends to contrast some of the *destructive lies* we are presented with from the enemy, as well as the world, with the light of God's truth regarding health-related trials.

At some point, we will all face an event involving pain, injury or disease requiring hospitalization, rehab and perhaps even long-term care. Some will encounter a terminal diagnosis or permanent disability. And, many of us will become caretakers.

As the enemy attempts to twist a health challenge into a faith crisis, we must keep our spiritual armor on. This book was written for those suffering, as well as their caregivers. It attempts to eliminate doubt by redirecting our attention to the strength, perseverance and peace found only in Jesus Christ. It also offers insight to the hope in, purpose of and benefits yielded from suffering.

Extra pages for notes have been provided in the back of this book for you to write your thoughts, prayers, scripture verses and more.

Come and draw near to the God of all comfort.

ACKNOWLEDGEMENTS

This devotional was written by drawing from real life interactions I have had over the years with my rehab patients during their Occupational Therapy treatments. It was also inspired by my own personal experiences during times of physical struggles, sickness and healing.

I am extremely thankful to all those who shared their faith, fears and doubts with me. I consider it a privilege to have been trusted through their trials, given the opportunity to share the gospel and pray with those who were open to it.

Most importantly, I thank my Lord and Savior, Jesus Christ — for everything.

DAY

One

Lie: "I would be afraid if I were you."

"God is our refuge and strength, A very present help in trouble. Therefore we will not fear, Even though the earth be removed, And though the mountains be carried into the midst of the sea; Though its waters roar and be troubled, Though the mountains shake with its swelling." (Psalm 46:1-3 NKJV)

When sudden illness, injury, or a new diagnosis comes without warning we must remember where our help comes from. Waves of fear can cause us to feel as if we are drowning in anxiety, causing us to needlessly panic.

The disciples also felt that fear of impending doom when a fast and furious storm came upon them while crossing the Sea of Galilee (Matthew 8:23-27). While waves of water swept over their boat, Jesus slept. Feeling helpless, the disciples screamed for Jesus to save them. Despite the fact the disciples had already witnessed Jesus perform miracles, they were still overcome with fear.

Jesus awoke, rebuked the winds and water, and all was calm. Jesus said, "You of little faith, why are you so afraid?" Jesus pointed out that their fear was related to their lack of faith, or trust, in Him.

Why then are we so afraid? Fear, which we all experience at times, is directly related to a lack of faith. When we experience doubt, God reassures us of His faithfulness through His word. He is completely trustworthy. God is with us in all the storms of life just as He was with the disciples. When we trust in Christ completely we exercise and strengthen our faith.

Therefore, we need to cry out to Jesus in faith. God is always with us, in control, and able to calm the waves of our storms whether we face pain, sickness, or even permanent disability. Nothing can separate us from the love of God which is in Christ Jesus our Lord. (Romans 8:39) Trust Jesus completely through faith. Give Him your burden.

No fear, just faith.

Recommended Reading: Psalm 27:1, Psalm 46

DAY Two

Lie: "God must be punishing you."

"My brethren, count it all joy when you fall into various trials, knowing that the testing of your faith produces patience. But let patience have its perfect work, that you may be perfect and complete, lacking nothing." (James 1:2-4 NKJV)

God's word says consider trials joy, not punishment. We are saved by grace through faith in Christ from the eternal punishment we deserve. Yet there are natural consequences for our choices, behavior and living in a fallen world with disease.

When facing sickness, we can choose to run in one of two opposite directions. We can choose to wallow in the misery of self-pity or we can focus on our relationship with the Lord who loves us. The joy of the Lord is forever. This joy is from the Holy Spirit, and is the evidence of salvation through Christ. (1 Thessalonians 1:6) He was bestowed upon us the day we accepted Christ. We can choose to delight in the eternal blessing we already have promise of, in good times and trials. Running the course with joy enables us to acquire endurance, building our spiritual muscles to stand up under pressure along the way. (Romans 5:3)

God desires not to destroy us but to save us from sin and refine us in the fire during the race of life. This is yet another way we grow in our faith, our trust in Christ, and become mature Christians lacking nothing in order to persevere in this world. From experience comes wisdom on how to deal with and press on through the next trial life brings. We must depend on the Lord. When others are encouraged by our perseverance we can then boast of the hope and strength found only in Christ.

There is joyful hope in knowing that almighty God, who is carrying us through our trials, is the same God at the finish line who one day will say, "Well done good and faithful servant."

Recommended Reading: Romans 5:1-5

DAY Three

Lie: "God doesn't understand your pain."

"He is despised and rejected by men, A Man of sorrows and acquainted with grief. And we hid, as it were, our faces from Him; He was despised, and we did not esteem Him. Surely He has borne our griefs and carried our sorrows; Yet we esteemed Him stricken, Smitten by God, and afflicted." (Isaiah 53:3-4 NKJV)

Let us try to imagine ourselves suffering what the Lord Jesus, God in a human flesh, endured on our behalf.

With bare skin exposed and hands tied to a tall pole the physical torment continues after a hands-on beating. The multi-tailed leather whip donned with pieces of metal and broken glass wraps around Jesus' back, digging deeply into soft flesh. Jesus remains silent. The soldier torturing Jesus pulls the whip back with all his might, torn flesh hanging from it. Now muscles are exposed, blood pouring out faster with each of the 39 excruciating blows.

After Jesus' scourging a robe is placed over His bloody body soaking up the liquid which begins to dry.

A crown of large thorns is thrust into Jesus' head, which has already been beaten beyond recognition. Human life is literally running out of Jesus. A massive wooden beam is placed on Jesus' open back to be carried to the place of our creator's death.

As Jesus carries the heavy beam, He grows weaker. The extreme blood loss is taking a toll. A man named Simon is called to help Jesus carry the beam. Jesus slowly makes it up the hill where more agonizing pain awaits.

The robe soaked in blood which has dried to Jesus' back is ripped off to reopen deep wounds. Jesus is placed upon a cross where spikes several inches long are driven through His wrists. Pain overwhelms Jesus while an even longer spike is driven through both of His feet, one on top of the other. The cross is lifted up and dropped into a deep hole in the ground.

Jesus' legs can't hold up His body, they are cramping and burning. Jesus' shoulders are dislocating. In order to breathe Jesus needs to push down on the nail in His feet.

Hours pass, it's so hard for Jesus to breathe, our Lord's heart is beating rapidly… His lungs are filling with fluid… Jesus is suffocating. Fluid is drowning Jesus' sinless, loving heart…

It is finished.

Jesus understands our pain.

Recommended Reading: 1 John 4:10

DAY

Four

Lie: "A loving God would not allow such suffering."

"Then the Lord said to Satan, "Have you considered My servant Job, that there is none like him on the earth, a blameless and upright man, one who fears God and shuns evil? And still he holds fast to his integrity, although you incited Me against him, to destroy him without cause." (Job 2:3 NKJV)

There are things that take place in the spiritual world of which we have no knowledge, yet they dramatically affect our lives. In Job's case, Satan had been roaming the earth for victims to assault just as he continues to do today. Job was unaware of the cause of his suffering the loss of his children and vast possessions. Despite his tragic loss, he worshipped God and held fast to his integrity.

Satan's second and more physical attack on Job, causing painful boils from head to toe, proved to be overwhelming. Great physical pain and suffering, as well as grief, now gripped Job. Job's anguish caused him to complain and question God.

After God's rebuke emphasizing His holy authority, Job is humbled and submits to God's sovereignty. Job repents of accusations against God, prays for his accusing friends, and is blessed by God more than before his turmoil began.

Sometimes our suffering is a consequence of our sin, or the sin of others, but not in Job's case. He was, without his knowledge, being tested by Satan. Satan wanted Job to lose his faith, curse God and turn from Him. Satan, the ruler of this world (John 12:31), continues to play the same game with us today.

Just like Job we can find ourselves complaining and questioning God's fairness in our troubles. We prefer life to be easy and trouble free. We are incapable of understanding God's ways. Yet we know from Job's experience that God is always in control, full of compassion, and is trustworthy when we don't understand our circumstances.

What God allows has a divine purpose.

Recommended Reading: Isaiah 55:8-13, John 16:33

DAY

Five

Lie: "Your God doesn't hear you."

"Hear my prayer, O Lord, and let my cry come to you. Do not hide your face from me in the day of my trouble; Incline your ear to me; In the day that I call, answer me speedily. For my days are consumed like smoke, and my bones are burned like a hearth. My heart is stricken and withered like grass, so that I forget to eat my bread. Because of the sound of my groaning my bones cling to my skin. I am like a pelican of the wilderness; I am like an owl of the desert." (Psalm 102:1-6 NKJV)

Our physical and emotional affliction can leave us feeling very weak and lonely, causing us to lose our appetite and feel like dried up, withered grass. Some of us have absolutely no one who cares to hear of our burdens or offer comfort. We are aching for the relief of a listening ear. The psalmist shares in the familiar pain of loneliness.

When we are in that place of desperation the most beneficial words we can speak are, "Hear my prayer, O Lord." We know that our cry goes to God and He will never hide His face from us. He is waiting to hear from us through prayer. Our relationship with our Heavenly Father is sustained with communication through prayer, His word, and worship.

God hears our prayers as He heard David's. (Psalm 18:6 NKJV) "In my distress I called upon the Lord, And cried out to my God; He heard my voice from His temple, And my cry came before Him, even to His ears."

Our help comes from God. (Psalm 121:1-2 NKJV) "I will lift up my eyes to the hills — From whence comes my help? My help comes from the Lord, Who made heaven and earth."

If we are honest with ourselves our prayer time usually increases during times of trouble. God knows how to get our attention and He wants to keep it. A beautiful result of our suffering can be a deeper, richer, more intimate prayer life with our Savior. Prayer has a way of redirecting our attention away from our circumstances and onto the one waiting to hear our cry for help. The one who loves and sustains us is the one we should constantly seek through regular prayer. In sickness and in health.

Our Heavenly Father is listening and waiting with open arms.

Run to Him, in Jesus' name.

Recommended Reading: Psalm 55:16-17

DAY

Lie: "You must have done something wrong."

"Now as Jesus passed by, He saw a man who was blind from birth. And His disciples asked Him saying, "Rabbi, who sinned, this man or his parents, that he was born blind?" Jesus answered, "Neither this man nor his parents sinned, but that the works of God should be revealed in him." (John 9:1-3 NKJV)

We live in a fallen world with disease where most of us, at one point or another, will suffer. Our suffering can very well be a direct result of our sin. Alcoholism can lead to liver failure, adultery to sexually transmitted disease, drugs to brain damage.

Sin was not the cause of the man's blindness in John 9. God had a specific purpose, so that the work of God would be displayed in the man's life. What an awesome demonstration of His power and love to all those watching.

God continues to this day to work in our lives in order to be glorified. Will He heal our diseases? That is for the Lord to know and for us to pray for, in faith, according to His will. He is able to heal, is in control, and will be glorified.

May we glorify Him not only when it's easy in our comfort, but in our pain, because of our love for Him. For we love Him, because He first loved us enough to open our spiritually blinded eyes to our need for repentance, leading to His curing salvation. Through His wounds we are healed and through our wounds may He be glorified.

Recommended Reading: Matthew 4:23-24

DAY
Seven

Lie: "There's no hope for this old body."

"For our citizenship is in heaven, from which we also eagerly wait for the Savior, the Lord Jesus Christ, who will transform our lowly body that it may be conformed to His glorious body, according to the working by which He is able even to subdue all things to Himself." (Philippians 3:20-21 NKJV)

Many frail seniors, as well as the sickly young, find themselves physically falling apart. Bones break easily, pipes back up, and body systems fail while hope fades. Being advanced in age can make new medical issues, as well as rehab, an overwhelming challenge. Many have overcome with renewed strength, while others lose hope and give up.

God designed our earthly bodies to bounce back in many ways, even those with high mileage. Under God's care we can work hard, persevere, and get well once again. When that is not God's will for us we can always depend on His promise of a glorified, resurrected body.

Our salvation through our Lord and Savior Jesus Christ seals the deal. (John 11:25-26 NKJV) "Jesus said to her, "I am the resurrection and the life. He who believes in Me, though he may die, he shall live. And whoever lives and believes in Me shall never die. Do you believe this?"

(Revelation 20:6 NKJV) "Blessed and holy is he who has part in the first resurrection. Over such the second death has no power, but they shall be priests of God and of Christ, and shall reign with Him a thousand years." Those of us who are saved by faith and die, are blessed with the promise of entering His kingdom.

We can trust God's word. We have the best to look forward to. How wonderful that will be when we are conformed to His glorious body. There will be no more pain, no more tears, no more suffering. We will enter into a body specially designed for eternal life with God.

We will drink in His peace, love and mercy, never to thirst again.

Recommend Reading: 1 Corinthians 15:35-54,
2 Corinthians 5:1-8

DAY

Eight

Lie: "God doesn't really answer prayer for healing."

"In those days Hezekiah was sick and near death. And Isaiah the prophet, the son of Amoz, went to him and said to him, "Thus says the LORD: 'Set your house in order, for you shall die, and not live."

Then he turned his face toward the wall, and prayed to the LORD, saying, "Remember now, O LORD, I pray, how I have walked before You in truth and with a loyal heart, and have done what was good in Your sight." And Hezekiah wept bitterly.

And it happened, before Isaiah had gone out into the middle court, that the word of the LORD came to him, saying, "Return and tell Hezekiah the leader of My people, Thus says the LORD, the God of David your father: "I have heard your prayer, I have seen your tears; surely I will heal you. On the third day you shall go up to the house of the LORD. And I will add to your days fifteen years. I will deliver you and this city from the hand of the king of Assyria; and I will defend this city for My own sake, and for the sake of My servant David." (2 Kings 20:1-6 NKJV)

When Hezekiah became ill to the point of death, and was told by Isaiah that God said Hezekiah was going to die, Hezekiah responded in prayer and supplication. God said Hezekiah was going to die yet Hezekiah still humbled himself before God. Hezekiah asked God to remember his loyalty and devotion to Him. God heard Hezekiah's prayer and saw his tears. The Lord blessed Hezekiah with a promise of fifteen more years of life on earth and delivered Jerusalem from the enemy.

God healed Hezekiah and defended the city for His namesake. In (Isaiah 38:10-20), we read what Hezekiah wrote of facing his death and how God responded by blessing him with 15 more years. When Hezekiah wrote of God's faithfulness it was made known to the coming generations. People saw that Hezekiah's thankfulness was demonstrated through worship in the house of the Lord all the days of his life. In this, God's loving heart, compassion, and magnificent works were glorified.

What glorious deeds He performs on our behalf. Tell everyone about the amazing things He does.

Recommended Reading: Isaiah 38:10-20

Nine

Lie: "If you could just walk again you would be whole."

"Then behold, men brought on a bed a man who was paralyzed, whom they sought to bring in and lay before Him. And when they could not find how they might bring him in, because of the crowd, they went up on the housetop and let him down with his bed through the tiling into the midst before Jesus.

When He saw their faith, He said to him, "Man, your sins are forgiven you."

And the scribes and the Pharisees began to reason, saying, "Who is this who speaks blasphemies? Who can forgive sins but God alone?"

But when Jesus perceived their thoughts, He answered and said to them, "Why are you reasoning in your hearts? Which is easier, to say, 'Your sins are forgiven you,' or to say, 'Rise up and walk'? But that you may know that the

Son of Man has power on earth to forgive sins" — He said to the man who was paralyzed, "I say to you, arise, take up your bed, and go to your house."

Immediately he rose up before them, took up what he had been lying on, and departed to his own house, glorifying God." (Luke 5:18-25 NKJV)

Scripture frequently reveals God's mighty power to heal our infirmities. We see in Luke chapter 5 how Jesus healed the paralytic who was brought to Him by his friends. They were all quite determined to see the Lord. Even though the crowd was too large to get through they made a way by lowering the paralytic down through the roof to the Lord. It must have taken a lot of effort to get the man up on the roof.

Before Jesus healed the man's physical burden He addressed an even greater need by forgiving the man's sin. The Lord not only demonstrated His ability to heal disabilities, but more importantly His unique authority to forgive us of our sin. Not man but God alone has the power to forgive sin.

Jesus wants to cleanse us of the spiritual sickness we harbor inside. God has the power to heal the most debilitating of burdens, our sin.

Cut the middle-man, go straight to God in Jesus' name and be made whole.

Recommended Reading: Acts 13:38-39, Romans 6:23

DAY

Ten

Lie: "God must have made a mistake
when he made me."

"For You formed my inward parts; You covered me in
my mother's womb. I will praise You, for I am fearfully
and wonderfully made; Marvelous are Your works, And
that my soul knows very well.
My frame was not hidden from You, When I was made
in secret, And skillfully wrought in the lowest parts of
the earth.
Your eyes saw my substance, being yet unformed. And
in Your book they all were written, The days fashioned
for me, When as yet there were none of them."
(Psalm 139:13-16 NKJV)

God is perfect, He doesn't make mistakes. He knit
each and every one of us together with great care and for
a purpose, His purpose. Not just the physically healthy
people in this world, but all of His creation.

When God gives us a heart for the sick and disabled
it is the beginning of a deeper revealing of His love for

all of us. God has revealed Himself to us in allowing the hurting and the defenseless to teach us who we are in Christ.

Through caring for those with special needs, God teaches us patience and humility while developing a deep compassion for others. He blesses us with a ministry. People with special needs are priceless gifts and have an extraordinary purpose here on earth in facilitating what God is growing in us, hearts of unconditional love. The things of this world lose their value and are replaced with the precious things of God.

By working together through physical and mental challenges, God's purpose for all of us unfolds.

Recommended Reading: Psalm 145:9-10

DAY

Eleven

Lie: "I can handle this myself."

"Thus the heavens and the earth, and all the host of them, were finished. And on the seventh day God ended His work which He had done, and He rested on the seventh day from all His work which He had done." (Genesis 2:1-2 NKJV)

In the book of Genesis, we read that God rested from all His work of creation. Then He sanctified, or set apart the Sabbath because He rested in it. Almighty God wasn't tired after all He had done, but we need to take heed of what God modeled for us to do. Since our work as caretakers can be ongoing we need to set apart time to rest and connect with God.

How many times have we told ourselves we should be able to do it all ourselves? Caring for an elderly parent, a special needs child or disabled spouse can be overwhelming and exhausting. No matter who you care for it's easy to fall into the self-inflicted trap of trying to do it all. It's impossible, unnecessary and potentially debilitating. Caring for a loved one all alone can lead to frustration, resentment and even depression.

Caregivers need to set aside pride, ask for help and actually accept it. It's a wise thing to do. Ask family, friends and fellow church members to give some of their time to help. Many folks are happy to help serve just as we serve our loved ones. There are also many home care services available in every community.

Make time for yourself to rest, not only on the Sabbath but during the week as well. Do something fun and get away for a while. Take a nap if possible and accept the rest God gives. Go for a walk and enjoy God's creation. Enjoy fellowship with a friend. Your call to serve will be there when you return.

We can't effectively serve others if we are burned-out. There is no cool drink to offer when the well is dried up. We need to be refilled by spending time with God, in fellowship with others, in prayer and drinking in His living water.

Let's face it, our Heavenly Father knows best. Even Jesus often took time from His ministry to be alone with God and pray. He enjoyed meals with friends. He slept.

Recommended Reading: Mark 2:27-28

DAY

Twelve

Lie: "Nothing good can come from suffering."

"And we know that all things work together for good to those who love God, to those who are the called according to His purpose." (Romans 8:28 NKJV)

In all things, good and bad, joyful and sorrowful, and in sickness or health, God works for our ultimate benefit. Of course, not everything that happens will be positive. Jesus promised trials. God is fulfilling His purpose in those of us who love God and are called by Him through faith in Jesus Christ. God is with us working for our earthly and eternal benefit by molding us into the image of Christ.

Remember that God is omniscient, all knowing. He knew in eternity past, long before He created us, who would come to Christ. His heart's desire has always been to have a close love relationship with each of us. He knew we would fall and need a savior who would suffer the ultimate sacrifice for us. The salvation of the world came through His suffering for us.

We too have to suffer at times. Yet, in the toughest times we can draw near to Him, and trust completely in His purpose which is beyond our understanding. We can persist through painful trials, growing more obedient while God is teaching, correcting, and blessing us with wisdom. We can have peace knowing that all of it is ultimately for our good, according to His purpose.

And, we will one day understand.

Recommended Reading: Psalm 100:4-5

DAY

Thirteen

Lie: "I don't need the church."

"Is anyone among you suffering? Let him pray. Is anyone cheerful? Let him sing psalms. Is anyone among you sick? Let him call for the elders of the church, and let them pray over him, anointing him with oil in the name of the Lord." (James 5:13-14 NKJV)

When we are hurting and feeling weak, we need to cry out to our Heavenly Father in prayer. Prayer is our direct line to God who is always listening for His children's voices, even when we don't know what to pray. (Romans 8:26) tells us that the person of the Holy Spirit which lives inside the born again Christian, helps us in our weakness and intercedes for us on our behalf with groaning too deep for words.

Are you having a good day? Are you feeling cheerful and perhaps on the mend? Sing psalms to the Lord and thank Him who shares in our joy as well as our sorrow.

Praise Him for another day of life.

We are so blessed not only to share our circumstances with our creator, but also with the body of Christ. The Lord created us to desire fellowship with other believers for our own good, and the good of the entire body. A physical body part doesn't function when removed from the body. As part of the body of Christ we gain support, encouragement, and a deeper connection with those who are like minded. Like the early church, we are able to share with other believers in all circumstances praying for each other, and fulfilling each other's needs.

The church's prayers over its fellow saints who are suffering with illness are powerful. Powerful to encourage the sad, to comfort the hurting, lift emotional burdens to facilitate healing…

And, request miracles.

Recommended Reading: 1 Corinthians 12:12-14

DAY

Fourteen

**Lie: "I am scared and
I have no one to help me through this."**

*"These things I have spoken to you while being present
with you. But the Helper, the Holy Spirit, whom the
Father will send in My name, He will teach you all
things, and bring to your remembrance all things that I
said to you. Peace I leave with you, My peace I give to
you; not as the world gives do I give to you. Let not
your heart be troubled, neither let it be afraid."
(John 14:25-27 NKJV)*

Jesus told the disciples the Holy Spirit was coming to
help them remember what Jesus had said and done. The
Holy Spirit helps us in the same way today to remember
God's truth.

While we make our way through the maze of doctors'
appointments, tests, surgeries, hospitalizations, rehab, and
all the stressful aspects of illness, we need to be in God's
word. The world's definition of peace is not synonymous

with God's. God said we would experience conflict, trials, wars, and everything that contradicts the world's version of peace.

Peace from Christ is a spiritual peace which surpasses human understanding. God gives it to us freely through the person of the Holy Spirit who lives inside us as believers. God's peace offers us courage in all our circumstances because we know He holds our lives in His hands.

Just as Christ said, we need not allow our hearts to be troubled or afraid in any situation we may encounter now or in the future. There is peace in the reality of salvation through faith in Christ.

Despite the enemy's desire to fill us with fear, Jesus has overcome the enemy. Praise God! As God's people, we are invited to receive the peace that the person of the Holy Spirit has for us.

He is with us always.

Recommended Reading: Philippians 4:6-7

DAY

Fifteen

Lie: "Death is the end of everything."

"For I consider that the sufferings of this present time are not worthy to be compared with the glory which shall be revealed in us. For the earnest expectation of the creation eagerly waits for the revealing of the sons of God." (Romans 8:18-19 NKJV)

When weakness attempts to overpower us, pain is relentless, and our afflictions appear to have taken over our lives, we should turn to our Heavenly Father and His wonderful promises. God will not only be strength in our weakness, comfort our pain, but will ultimately glorify us in the life to come. Physical death is the beginning of eternal life for those in Christ.

Those who are wise to admit sin, repent, and accept the free gift of grace by the blood of Christ will be sinless and holy in heaven. (Revelation 22:4 NKJV) "They shall see His face, and His name shall be on their foreheads." We will be able to gaze into God's eyes and live! This is just the beginning of the rest of our eternal lives.

Scripture states despite how high our present sufferings tower over us, they are not worth comparing to what eternity has for us. Nothing compares to the hope of the future glory to be revealed in us. We are unable to comprehend how awesome it will be. (Daniel 12:3 NKJV) "Those who are wise shall shine like the brightness of the firmament, and those who turn many to righteousness like the stars forever and ever."

Even all of creation, which is subject to decay in this sinful world, is longing to be transformed. If all of creation waits eagerly for us to be revealed, how much more can we anticipate our own heavenly metamorphosis?

Let us rejoice in the promise of eternal life to come.

Recommended Reading: Romans 6:4-6

DAY

Sixteen

**Lie: "He is such a great doctor,
you can put your faith in him."**

*"And in the thirty-ninth year of his reign, Asa became
diseased in his feet, and his malady was severe; yet in
his disease, he did not seek the Lord, but the
physicians." (2 Chronicles 16:12 NKJV)*

Scripture tells us that when Asa became Judah's king
the land experienced ten years of peace. Asa did what was
right in the eyes of the Lord. Asa removed the pagan
altars, temple prostitutes, and told the people of Judah to
return to the Lord God of their ancestors. God gave them
rest because they sought the Lord.

Asa cried out to the Lord depending on God to cover
them in battle. When Asa returned victorious, the prophet
Azariah addressed Asa and all the people, "And he went
out to meet Asa, and said to him: "Hear me, Asa, and all
Judah and Benjamin. The LORD is with you while you are
with Him. If you seek Him, He will be found by you; but

if you forsake Him, He will forsake you." (2 Chronicles 15:2. NKJV)

Asa then removed all the idols from Judah and Benjamin. He renovated the altar of the Lord in front of the temple. The people returned to the Lord, sought Him with all their hearts, and God was found by them.

Israel's King Baasha went to war against Judah and built a city to deny access to Asa. Instead of depending on God in that situation, Asa depended on a pagan king to help him. The seer Hanani reminded Asa that God shows Himself strong for those whose hearts are completely His. Due to Asa's foolishness of not depending on God, there would be war from then on. When Asa was rebuked by God through Hanani, Asa grew angry, threw Hanani into prison, and mistreated his people.

In Asa's later years he developed a disease in his feet. He didn't seek the Lord but placed his faith in the physicians. Despite the severity of the disease, perhaps a merciful opportunity to repent, trust was again placed in man instead of God.

Of course, we need medical help when we are ill. But, do we seek the Lord first in our pain or do we turn to man only? In times of sickness, just as Asa did, many Christians have more faith in the doctors God created than the creator Himself. God is the one who is all powerful, equipping doctors with knowledge and talents to help the sick. It is God who chooses to work through them according to His will.

If God rebukes us as He did with Asa we must not abandon God but recognize His unfailing love for us, repent, and earnestly seek Him. God's merciful correction is what we all need to stay on the path of righteousness, growing up in Christ. We must not let His mercies turn us away but instead cause us to draw nearer to Him with our whole hearts.

Now is the time to repent and place our faith back where it belongs in the living God. The Lord is our great physician. When we seek Him, He is found.

Recommended Reading: Deuteronomy 4:29

DAY

Seventeen

Lie: "God doesn't care about my problems."

"Therefore humble yourselves under the mighty hand of God, that He may exalt you in due time, casting all your care upon Him, for He cares for you. Be sober, be vigilant; because your adversary the devil walks about like a roaring lion, seeking whom he may devour. Resist him, steadfast in the faith, knowing that the same sufferings are experienced by your brotherhood in the world. But may the God of all grace, who called us to His eternal glory by Christ Jesus, after you have suffered a while, perfect, establish, strengthen, and settle you. To Him be the glory and the dominion forever and ever. Amen." (1 Peter 5:6-11 NKJV)

When we are sick, suffering, and feel pushed to our limit, we can cast our anxiety on the Lord. The Lord wants us to come to Him as we are with a humble and repentant heart so He can care for us. God loves us more than we are capable of understanding. When we cast our concerns on Him we throw it on the Lord and it is no longer ours. The Lord is the one who is truly in control of our situation.

Our job is to be alert and focused on God not our problems. In the midst of physical suffering, when we can be most vulnerable, it is vital to be strong spiritually and not allow the accuser to take us down. The prowling lion persistently seeks to devour us and knows when we are feeling alone and weak. We don't need to be easy prey for his attacks. Trusting the Lord, staying in prayer, worship, the word of God, and fellowship with other believers will keep us strong standing firm in our faith.

Remember after we have suffered for a while, God promises to make us stronger. (Hebrews 12:7-13) While the enemy may attempt to kick us when we are down, the Lord is stretching, growing, and strengthening us because he loves us.

So, stay sober of mind, faithful, walking humbly with eyes focused on Christ every step of the way.

Give Him your problems for He does care.

Recommended Reading: Psalm 36:7, Psalm 55:22

DAY

Eighteen

Lie: "There is no hope for me."

"Hope deferred makes the heart sick, But when the desire comes, it is a tree of life." (Proverbs 13:12 NKJV)

When our hope is fading our hearts can grow sick, or depressed. Depression longs to take over mind, body, and spirit resulting in unnecessary emotional, physical and spiritual pain. More people than ever, including Christians, succumb to some form of depression be it acute or chronic.

The enemy and the world desire to steal our hope causing us to sink into a psychological pit of despair. As the world places its hope in money, achievements, and power, among other temporary things, as Christians we need not ever lose hope. Our hope is an eternal one wrapped up in love. God offers spiritual restoration.

Hope can be described as anticipation, optimism,

promise, confidence, and faith. (Hebrews 11:1 NKJV) says "Now faith is the substance of things hoped for, the evidence of things not seen." We are assured in God's word to us of the things we cannot yet see.

Scripture tells of a tree of life, the spiritual hope or longing literally fulfilled. (Genesis 2:9 NKJV) "And out of the ground the LORD God made every tree grow that is pleasant to the sight and good for food. The tree of life was also in the midst of the garden, and the tree of the knowledge of good and evil." The tree of life in the Garden of Eden provided eternal life from which we were separated through our sin. (Revelation 2:7 NKJV) "He who has an ear, let him hear what the Spirit says to the churches. To him who overcomes I will give to eat from the tree of life, which is in the midst of the Paradise of God." We have overcome by placing our faith in He who has overcome death, Jesus Christ.

(Revelation 22:14 NKJV) "Blessed are those who do His commandments, that they may have the right to the tree of life, and may enter through the gates into the city." Our robes are washed in the blood of Jesus Christ for the forgiveness of our sin. Therefore, placing our hope in the Lord, through faith, we receive God's free gift of grace and will enter into heaven and gain access to the tree of life, eternal life.

We need not allow our hearts to be sickened by a lack of hope. We have a living hope through the resurrection of Christ! Our reservation in heaven is sealed and no one can take that away from us. As we walk through this life on earth we are never alone, God is with us. Although we may be tested by fire through trials, we should continue to praise and honor our Lord for the hope He gives freely by His sacrifice.

Drown out depression with the living water of Christ. Feast on the daily bread of His word which fills and sustains us.

Keep hope focused on the cross and do not let your eyes deviate from it. See the blood flowing down the cross washing our robes clean thereby fulfilling our deepest longing, the longing of unconditional love and forgiveness that only God can provide.

His everlasting, healing love is all the hope we need.

Recommended Reading: 2 Thessalonians 2:16-17

DAY Nineteen

Lie: "You might as well just end it."

"For I know the thoughts that I think toward you, says the LORD, thoughts of peace and not of evil, to give you a future and a hope." (Jeremiah 29:11 NKJV)

Just as the Lord spoke to Israel about a future and a hope, he speaks to us. The Lord clearly says he has thoughts of peace toward us, and plans to give us a future and a hope. God provides His plan, we seek Him, He reveals His plan and we have peace. We live with a hope and a purpose.

The enemy also has plans for us that include an abundance of everything that contradicts God's plans. God's voice convicts us when we sin but Satan's voice condemns us. Scripture describes Satan's punishing voice for what it really is. (John 8:44 NKJV) "He was a murderer from the beginning, and does not stand in the truth, because there is no truth in him. When he speaks a lie, he speaks from his own resources, for he is a liar and the father of it."

The father of lies whispers condemning thoughts of

weakness, worthlessness, and the inability to go on. He can burden us so heavily with lies that we are unable to see past our present situation. He will attempt to convince us that our lives aren't worth anything, we aren't good enough, and can no longer deal with life so we would be better off ending it all. These words come from a murdering liar and couldn't be farther from the truth of God.

The truth is our value isn't based on our circumstances. Losing a job, possessions, family members, being bullied, rejected, alone, brain damaged, addicted to drugs, or terminally ill — no matter what tribulation we find ourselves in the midst of only God is qualified to do an appraisal of our lives. He is the one who gave us life and every single life is a precious treasure to him. We are so cherished by God He gave His life for us.

(Ephesians 2:10 NKJV) "For we are His workmanship, created in Christ Jesus for good works, which God prepared beforehand that we should walk in them."

We are His workmanship, a beautiful work of art, His jewels, His beloved gems created anew in Jesus. We are our father's priceless sons and daughters.

Let us turn our ears from deceptive lies and turn to God's truth.

In Christ, there is peace, receive it.

In Christ, we are loved, run into His arms.

In Christ, there is a purpose for living, embrace it.

Recommended Reading: Romans 8:37-39, Psalm 34:17-19

DAY

Twenty

Lie: "There is no hell."

"For God so loved the world that He gave His only begotten Son, that whoever believes in Him should not perish but have everlasting life. For God did not send His Son into the world to condemn the world, but that the world through Him might be saved." (John 3:16-17 NKJV)

Contrary to popular belief, there is a very real place called hell. If we barely open our eyes we will see that evil is all around us. You can believe that the devil, demons, and hell are very real. The greatest form of pain and suffering is not of this world but reserved in eternal hell for the devil, his demons, and those who reject God's love, grace, and mercy.

(Matthew 13:40-43NKJV) "Therefore as the tares are gathered and burned in the fire, so it will be at the end of this age. The Son of Man will send out His angels, and they will gather out of His kingdom all things that offend, and those who practice lawlessness, and will cast them into the furnace of fire. There will be wailing and gnashing of teeth. Then the righteous will shine forth as the sun in the kingdom of their Father. He who has ears to hear, let him hear!"

Whoever has ears, let them hear that the tares are those who deny the God who loves them and reject the free gift of grace offered through His son Jesus Christ. What suffering awaits those who refuse to admit their sin and repent.

We all have sin and are unable live up to God's perfect standard. The law clearly revealed our sin to us. Our sin has separated us from a holy and perfect God. There is no amount of good deeds we can do to erase our sin and renew our relationship with God. God demanded that blood be shed for the forgiveness of sin.

We are forgiven through believing in our hearts and confessing with our mouths, that Christ died shedding His blood for our sin, was resurrected on the third day, and accepting Him as our Lord and Savior. (Romans 10:9) We are righteous in the eyes of God because of what Jesus did for us. We are saved from not only our sin, but from eternal darkness, weeping, and torment.

Because of God's love for us we can be saved unto a life of living hope in this world and one of peace in heaven where there will be no more pain, tears, or suffering.

Recommended Reading: John 14:2-4

DAY

Twenty-One

Lie: "Your God has left you in the dark."

"You are the light of the world. A city that is set on a hill cannot be hidden. Nor do they light a lamp and put it under a basket, but on a lamp stand, and it gives light to all who are in the house. Let your light so shine before men, that they may see your good works and glorify your Father in heaven." (Matthew 5:14-16 NKJV)

Super hero movies are more popular than ever these days. With all the evil in the world today it can be a fun escape to watch the "bigger than life" characters triumph over the bad guys.

I am often asked by our teenage son what super powers I would prefer to possess.

God Almighty has already equipped every Christian with the super power of His Holy Spirit. Even though we were once darkness, He hasn't left us in the dark (Ephesians 5:8-14). We have the light of God inside us.

He has blessed us with the opportunity to be part of a special team's mission — the great commission of taking the gospel to all nations.

Jesus said we are the light of the world and should let our light shine before all people. Our testimony of God's unconditional love and saving grace, especially in the midst of suffering, is an eye-opening light to those still living in the dark.

(John 8:12 NKJV) "Then Jesus spoke to them again, saying, "I am the light of the world. He who follows Me shall not walk in darkness, but have the light of life."

God is glorified when we are at peace during trials…

Comforted by God's word when in pain…

Hopeful for the future when confronted with a disability…

A godly response in our suffering is an impressive witness to the saving power of the grace of God.

Recommended Reading: Philippians 2:14-16

DAY Twenty-Two

Lie: "It's impossible to love such nasty people."

"But the fruit of the Spirit is love, joy, peace, longsuffering, kindness, goodness, faithfulness, gentleness, self-control. Against such there is no law." (Galatians 5:22-23 NKJV)

Whether you are a professional caregiver such as a nurse, nurse's assistant, doctor, therapist, companion or family member caring for a relative at home, you have a challenging job to say the least.

We know in our hearts we couldn't do this alone from our own resources. We can do nothing apart from Christ (John 15:5). God equips us for such a servant's task.

We as believers in Christ received the person of the Holy Spirit when we first believed and surrendered to the Lord. What an amazing thing our Heavenly Father has done by blessing us with His Holy Spirit to live in us, guide us and transform us.

The characteristics of Christ that the Spirit grows in us, such as love, are awesome rewards in themselves. I thought I knew what love was before I began serving strangers who were suffering. I knew the kind of love I have toward my family and friends. It's easy to love those who love us in return. Then I met people who weren't always so happy to see me enter their hospital or nursing home room.

When we made a choice for Christ we chose love. We accepted God's unconditional love for us along with the task of extending His healing ministry to others. When we made a commitment to serve we put our hearts on the line to be broken, remolded and made new. In that sometimes painful process, we are blessed with hearts that overflow with devotion, compassion and tenderness for the sick and suffering.

For all the hard working, compassionate caregivers who are up to their knees in all the unpleasant bodily fluids you can name, or faced with frustrating, demanding and difficult people to care for, please remember that God is right beside you guiding you through it. His heart overflows as you follow His example. You may be the only example of Christ's love your patient or family member will ever witness.

When you are emotionally and physically spent take a quiet moment alone wherever you can and close your eyes. Go before the throne of God and pray. Remember Christ bleeding out His love on the cross for us and those we serve.

Pray for the Holy Spirit to resuscitate and refill the love of God in your heart to overflowing.

And, when people compliment you and say it takes a special person to do your job tell them it takes an AWESOME God to do it through you.

Recommended Reading: Matthew 22:36-39

Twenty-Three

Lie: "Christians use their religion as a crutch when they are suffering."

"Even so we, when we were children, were in bondage under the elements of the world. But when the fullness of the time had come, God sent forth His Son, born of a woman, born under the law, to redeem those who were under the law, that we might receive the adoption as sons. And because you are sons, God has sent forth the Spirit of His Son into your hearts, crying out, "Abba, Father!" Therefore you are no longer a slave but a son, and if a son, than an heir of God through Christ." (Galatians 4:3-7 NKJV)

Religion is defined as an organized system of beliefs, ceremonies and rules used to worship a god or group of gods. Ceremonies and good works must be abundant in order to earn points and outweigh sin with the gods of false religion. If enough is accomplished, by man's definition, we can work our way up to acceptance, reward and maybe even deity. Religion is a futile climb up an infinite ladder of good deeds that ultimately glorify our own efforts.

Contrary to the world's many false religions, the truth of God's word reveals that instead of needing to work our way up for acceptance by God, His love for us caused Him to send His Son down to earth to save us from our sin in order to have a right relationship with Him. Jesus willingly left His heavenly throne to testify to the truth of who God really is and to save us from our sin that had separated us from God. Jesus shed His own innocent blood for us so we could escape the punishment we all deserve which no amount of good deeds can erase. (Isaiah 53:6 NKJV) "All we like sheep have gone astray; We have turned, every one, to his own way; And the LORD has laid on Him the iniquity of us all." Now that's love, not religion.

It is at that moment when we admit our sin, turn from it, and accept the free gift of God's grace and forgiveness through Christ's sacrifice that we enter into a real love relationship with our Heavenly Father. There is no "to do" list or ladder to climb. Jesus' blood paid the price for us. Jesus is the bridge between us and our loving Father God who is waiting with open arms. And, there is more than enough love for everyone.

In (John 10:1-8) Jesus tells the religious leaders that He is the good shepherd and we are His sheep. He is the gate to God the Father and whoever enters through Him will be saved. And we will come in and go out and find pasture. Jesus is our mighty, loving and compassionate shepherd king leading us, His sheep, through life and ultimately into eternity.

God's love is not a man-made crutch that simply transfers the weight of the burden from our legs to our arms where we are still in control. God's unfailing love lifts us up onto His shoulders and carries us through every valley in life.

Have you entered into a relationship with the one who loves you?

Recommended Reading: Psalm 23

DAY Twenty-Four

Lie: "This disease will make life miserable."

"Blessed be the God and Father of our Lord Jesus Christ, the Father of mercies and God of all comfort, who comforts us in all our tribulation, that we may be able to comfort those who are in any trouble, with the comfort with which we ourselves are comforted by God." (2 Corinthians 1:3-4 NKJV)

In verse 4, the tribulation Paul was experiencing was intense pressure. Paul's efforts were constantly threatened. In 2 Corinthians 1:8-10, Paul was almost killed for spreading the gospel.

A chronic or progressive disease can be just as relentless as the problems Paul faced. Just as with Paul, God doesn't allow it to destroy us. Our God is the father of compassion and God of all comfort.

Compassion is not only feeling sorrow for someone in their affliction but a desire to alleviate the suffering.

When we cry out to Him, God moves right in and comforts us. In the midst of suffering, God strengthens us and gives us the courage we need to go on with bravery and face what lies ahead.

There is tremendous comfort and rejuvenation found in meditating on the character of God. Our Heavenly Father is all powerful, all knowing and everywhere. He is the definition of what all our hearts yearn for including goodness, love, compassion and mercy. These are just a few of the perfect attributes of the amazing God who loved us before He created us. His spirit envelopes us like a holy blanket wrapping us in peace beyond human comprehension. That's why bathing ourselves in the word of God transforms misery to relief, frustration to encouragement, and downheartedness to hopefulness.

After we have received the comfort of the Lord which strengthens and invigorates us we are then able to do the same for others who are suffering the same trial. The most effective comfort a person can offer another is from a genuine understanding of having already walked miles in the same shoes.

So, praise be to our compassionate Heavenly Father, the God of all comfort. For His word gives us life, builds us up and reveals His glorious purpose for our lives.

Recommended Reading: Psalm 119:49-50

DAY
Twenty-Five

Lie: "I know, I read the gospels growing up."

"You believe that there is one God. You do well. Even the demons believe — and tremble!" (James 2:19 NKJV)

Knowledge is the acquaintance with facts, truths or principles as from study or investigation. The demons have the book knowledge as well as the ability to give an eye witness account to the truth of who God the Father, Jesus Christ and the Holy Spirit are. They have seen, heard and understand the doctrine, yet they are not saved.

There are many people who believe that because their parents are Christians, they are too, through association. Many believe because they attended Sunday school growing up that they are right with God. There are even some that can recite any scripture forward and back again, but this too is simply book knowledge without saving faith.

This is where the beauty of suffering comes in to save

a life. Yes, suffering a serious injury, illness or deadly disease can be very revealing and truly healing.

Physical pain, alongside the loss of our functional independence, has a way of exposing our human frailty.

Our prideful self-sufficiency will discover we need help from others.

Our fear of the unknown highlights our lack of control over our lives.

In our weakness, helplessness and frustration we realize our mere knowledge of God will not comfort us in our pain, give us hope or strength. What we desperately need is to be held in His loving arms.

The Pharisees of Jesus' time could recite scripture, loved religious rituals and were considered moral authorities. Yet they lacked spiritual transformation. They "knew of" God, but didn't know Him. They had no real love for God in their hearts.

Just as Jesus told the Pharisee Nicodemus, "Most assuredly, I say to you, unless one is born again, he cannot see the kingdom of God." (John 3:3NKJV)

To be born again means to be "born from above." This comes from God. It's a spiritual transformation made by the Holy Spirit through faith in Jesus Christ. The born-again Christian receives the gift of eternal life and becomes a child of God. According to Jesus Christ there is no other kind of Christian.

With most of us it takes some intense suffering for us to admit our real need for God. It is in the depths of our suffering that we long for not only physical relief, but forgiveness of our spiritual sickness — sin.

It is in this place that the word of God transitions from ink on a page to life everlasting.

Recommended Reading: 1 John 5:1

DAY Twenty-Six

Lie: "There is no way out of this addiction."

"No temptation has overtaken you except such as is common to man; but God is faithful, who will not allow you to be tempted beyond what you are able, but with the temptation will also make the way of escape, that you may be able to bear it." (1 Corinthians 10:13 NKJV)

It's probably safe to say people don't grow up with the intention of becoming an alcoholic or drug addict. Drugs and alcohol are some of those things many are tempted with because they appear harmless at first. That's the deception which can lead to addiction.

In (James 1:12-15) he speaks of how we can be tempted in life, drawn away by our own desires and enticed, and when desire has conceived, it gives birth to sin, and sin grows up bringing forth death. It's a gradual process that can lead to death, both spiritual and physical.

But we don't need to die in our sin, because God is faithful. Despite foolish life choices God will accept us the way we are right now. We don't need to get cleaned up first. He will do all the sanctifying. Jesus Christ came for the down and out, the sick, those in need of a physician. He came to heal our souls through His gift of grace. Healing is a choice we all need to make.

Simply...
- Believe that Christ died for our sin and God raised Him on the third day.
- Ask for His forgiveness and repent — turn away from sin.
- Receive the free gift of grace and follow Jesus as Lord.

"Therefore, if anyone is in Christ, he is a new creation; old things have passed away; behold, all things have become new." (2 Corinthians 5:17 NKJV)

Yes, even believers can fall back into drugs and alcohol. Then it's time to rededicate ourselves back to the Lord. Get back on the narrow road that leads to life. If we stumble and fall, we get back up. He will not allow us to be tempted beyond what we are able to handle — we will be able to bear the temptation and walk away straight toward Christ. We must choose between temptation and the way out.

Jesus Christ is the way out from temptation. The only way, truth and life there is.

Recommended Reading: 1 Corinthians 6:19-20

DAY

Twenty-Seven

Lie: "The prognosis isn't good."

"Therefore we do not lose heart. Even though our outward man is perishing, yet the inward man is being renewed day by day. For our light affliction, which is but for a moment, is working for us a far more exceeding and eternal weight of glory, while we do not look at the things which are seen, but at the things which are not seen. For the things which are seen are temporary, but the things which are not seen are eternal." (2 Corinthians 4:16-18 NKJV)

The apostle Paul knew what it meant to suffer. Paul had suffered a great deal of persecution while spreading the gospel including near death beatings, being imprisoned, shipwrecked and stoned. Yet, Paul described extreme hardships as light or weightless compared to the weight or heaviness of the future glory we will experience in heaven.

Progressive diseases such as ALS, MS and Parkinson's, just to name a few, can be overwhelming, heavy burdens to bear. While living in this world, in these physically declining bodies, we can become discouraged knowing it only gets more difficult physically as time goes on.

Yet, during these times God is renewing our souls, day by day. We are new creations maturing and growing up in Christ. We are being conformed into His likeness.

To refer to such adversity as "light" sounds heartless. Paul's description is not an attempt to trivialize aging or the attacks and beatings he encountered, but in comparison magnify the glory to come. Indeed, these relentless disease processes are also temporary and light in intensity compared to the glorious, immortal splendor that awaits us for all of eternity. There simply are no words to contrast the afflictions of this life with unspeakable glory.

While we may suffer a little while in the body, we look forward with great anticipation to the indescribable splendor to come. And, as our souls are being renewed, we may even catch a glimpse of His brilliant glory.

Recommended Reading: Romans 15:13

DAY Twenty-Eight

Lie: "The elderly are just a worthless burden to society."

"The silver-haired head is a crown of glory, If it is found in the way of righteousness." (Proverbs 16:31 NKJV)

We are born into this world helpless, at the mercy of others. We grow into teenagers, gain a bit of knowledge, and suddenly we think ourselves smarter than our parents. Years flow into adulthood, and if we are honest, we realize the older we get the less we really know.

If we are blessed with a long life in the Lord, we have attained Godly wisdom through life's experiences. And yes, we may find ourselves physically helpless once again at the mercy of others.

Much of today's society views the older, sickly and broken-down adult as a non-productive burden. Many are personally attacked in every way with family members lying in wait for their financial inheritance while missing out on the real treasure older adults have to share.

While the enemy strikes hard when we are down and feeling weak, God lifts up, values highly and protects. As children of God we must continually seek the truth of God's word. Our Heavenly Father has good plans for us our entire lives. A person is just as priceless in old age as in childhood.

Scripture clearly states that old age is a crown of glory for those who pursue Godly wisdom and righteousness. A crown of glory!

The older adult is cherished by God as a precious jewel the father has shaped over the years through good times and trials, sickness and health, from vibrant youth to fragile old age. They are equipped with a wealth of understanding to share with the younger, less experienced generation. And, God says that wisdom is "far more precious than gold."

To those believers advanced in years wisdom has accrued for times such as these. Aging souls with a wellspring of faith are valuable gifts which deserve respect and adoration. You are still used by God. Even those who are unable to speak or move can pray.

Be bold.

Share faith, giving abundantly from the wealth of maturity God has awarded.

God's not done yet.

Recommended Reading: Psalm 92

DAY
Twenty-Nine

Lie: "I'll believe it when I see it."

"Then as He entered a certain village, there met Him ten men who were lepers, who stood afar off. And they lifted up their voices and said, "Jesus, Master, have mercy on us!" So when He saw them, He said to them, "Go, show yourselves to the priests." And so it was that as they went, they were cleansed. And one of them, when he saw that he was healed, returned, and with a loud voice glorified God, and fell down on his face at His feet, giving Him thanks. And he was a Samaritan. So Jesus answered and said, "Were there not ten cleansed? But where are the nine? Were there not any found who returned to give glory to God except this foreigner?" And He said to him, "Arise, go your way. Your faith has made you well." (Luke 17:12-19 NKJV)

The lepers obeyed Him, believing what Jesus said before it even happened. That is trusting in the word of God. Then they were healed. Yet only one went back to thank God.

As followers of Christ we must ask ourselves when the going gets tough, when we are in pain, do we trust Him at His word and respond in obedience to what He is telling us to do? Or, do we need to see evidence of the outcome before we move on His word?

We need not fall prey to the enemy, or the world, trying to instill a lack of confidence in the one who never leaves us or forsakes us. "Jesus Christ is the same yesterday, today and forever." (Hebrews 13:8 NKJV)

He still heals according to His will, and comforts while offering real peace through relationship with Him. The result of our obedience to His will isn't necessarily seen immediately or even at all in this life. Draw near to Him, be patient and trust.

If we are healed, get stronger, or go into remission, do we openly praise the one responsible as the Samaritan did? He threw himself at the feet of Jesus and praised Him with a loud voice. Everyone in the vicinity was sure to hear the truth of His power to heal.

And, if we are not healed do we praise Him openly for who He is?

Trust in His strength before it comes.

Trust in His sovereign promises with obedient faith.

And glorify Him who is full of mercy and love so all the world can hear.

Recommend Reading: Proverbs 3:5

DAY

Thirty

Lie: "I am too weak."

"I know how to be abased, and I know how to abound. Everywhere and in all things I have learned both to be full and to be hungry, both to abound and to suffer need. I can do all things through Christ who strengthens me." (Philippians 4:12-13 NKJV)

In Philippians 4, Paul speaks of his experience living with humble means as well as abundance. He knew what it was like to withstand great difficulty. He had been through a multitude of life threatening adversities. He had been beaten, thrown into prison and gone without food. He also came to appreciate abundance and to be full.

Paul states that everywhere and in all things, he learned how to abound and suffer need. In every situation he faced, he was content. Everywhere he went he learned where his strength really came from. The Greek word for strengthen means "to put power in." Christ put this supernatural power in him to remain humble, and to persevere everywhere and in all things during his life.

Our lives too can unexpectedly change in an instant. Accidents happen every day leaving many with a permanent, life altering injury. This is where our spiritual rubber meets the crossroads of human limitations and a limitless God. On whom shall we depend? In our weakness where does our strength come from?

In one simple verse our complete and required sustenance of life is summed up. We need not try to derive strength from ourselves, we are unable. We have Christ the omnipotent, all powerful. Our all mighty Messiah will give us the necessary tenacity to get through every life-changing circumstance. He gives generously of His patience, strength, endurance and heavenly perspective to appreciate His endless mercy through our challenges. He gently lifts our heads up to face another day.

In His strength, we are sustained.

In His strength, we can start anew.

In His strength, we are made whole.

Recommended Reading: Psalm 121, Isaiah 40:27-31

DAY
Thirty-One

Lie: "This giant I am facing is too big for me."

"So it was, when the Philistine arose and came and drew near to meet David, that David hurried and ran toward the army to meet the Philistine." (1 Samuel 17:48 NKJV)

In order to settle a battle between the Philistines and Israelites, the Philistine giant, Goliath, proposed a one-on-one fight to the death. When the shepherd boy David heard of this challenge, he ran to meet and destroy the nearly 10-foot warrior.

David's courage came from his knowledge of who God is and how he had equipped David in the past when taking down lions and bears. David remembered how God worked in his life before facing Goliath. He knew God went before him in every situation just as He does for us.

Although it may appear so, our battles are not with the physical ailments or the disabilities we face.

"Finally, my brethren, be strong in the Lord and in the power of His might. Put on the whole armor of God, that you may be able to stand against the wiles of the devil. For we do not wrestle against flesh and blood, but against principalities, against powers, against the rulers of the darkness of this age, against spiritual hosts of wickedness in the heavenly places." (Ephesians 6:10-12 NKJV).

The enemy will use the physical to tear us down. He is the father of lies, seeking to destroy us spiritually in the hope of us turning from God, falling to disobedience, and ultimately descending into the abyss of hopelessness and defeat.

We need not fear.

The truth of God's word equips us to face any giant with the same confidence of David. Thus, we must don the armor of Christian soldiers.

"Therefore take up the whole armor of God, that you may be able to withstand in the evil day, and having done all to stand. Stand therefore, having girded your waist with truth, having put on the breastplate of righteousness, and having shod your feet with the preparation of the gospel of peace; above all, taking the shield of faith with which you will be able to quench all the fiery darts of the wicked one. And take the helmet of salvation, and the sword of the Spirit, which is the word of God; praying always with all prayer and supplication in the Spirit, being watchful to this end with all perseverance and supplication for all the saints." (Ephesians 6:13-18 NKJV)

We will stand wearing our spiritual armor. We must never take it off.

Truth: "Jesus said to him, "I am the way, the truth and the life. No one comes to the Father except through Me." (John 14:6 NKJV)

Jesus is the truth.

Righteousness: "But now the righteousness of God apart from the law is revealed, being witnessed by the Laws and the Prophets, even the righteousness of God, through faith in Jesus Christ, to all and on all who believe." (Romans 3:21-22 NKJV)

Through the blood of Christ, we stand righteous before God.

Gospel of Peace: "For God so loved the world that He gave His only begotten Son, that whoever believes in Him should not perish but have everlasting life." (John 3:16 NKJV)

Through Christ we have peace with God.

Shield of Faith: "Trust in the Lord with all your heart, and lean not on your own understanding; in all your ways acknowledge Him, and He shall direct your paths." (Proverbs 3:5-6 NKJV)

Faith is complete trust in God and His word.

Helmet of Salvation: "My sheep hear My voice, and I know them, and they follow Me. And I give them eternal life, and they shall never perish; neither shall anyone snatch them out of My hand. My Father, who has given them to Me, is greater than all; and no one is able to snatch them out of My Father's hand. I and My Father are one." (John 10:27-30 NKJV)

Our salvation is eternally protected through Christ.

The Sword of the Spirit Which Is the Word of God: "In the beginning was the Word, and the Word was with God, and the Word was God. He was in the beginning with God." (John 1:1-2 NKJV)

Jesus is the Word and God.

Praying Always with All Prayer and Supplication in the Spirit: "Rejoice always, pray without ceasing, in everything give thanks; for this is the will of God in Christ Jesus for you." (1 Thessalonians 5:16-18 NKJV) We pray frequently, in submission to God's will, persistently for all believers in Jesus' name.

In good times and through seasons of great suffering we must simply, consistently, wrap ourselves up in Jesus Christ.

He is our mighty armor, our loving savior, our great physician.

Recommended Reading: Psalm 27

If this book has been a blessing,
I would like to hear from you!

Please send me an email at:
M.A.Pasquale316@gmail.com

Notes

Made in the USA
Monee, IL
10 November 2019